50 Sizzling Summer BBQ Recipes

By: Kelly Johnson

Table of Contents

- Classic BBQ Baby Back Ribs
- Grilled Garlic Butter Shrimp Skewers
- Honey-Glazed BBQ Chicken Wings
- Smoky BBQ Pulled Pork Sliders
- Sweet and Tangy Grilled Pineapple Rings
- BBQ Brisket with Homemade Rub
- Cajun-Spiced Grilled Corn on the Cob
- Maple-Bourbon BBQ Salmon Fillets
- Chipotle-Lime Grilled Pork Chops
- Zesty BBQ Jackfruit Sandwiches
- BBQ Bacon-Wrapped Jalapeño Poppers
- Herb-Grilled Flat Iron Steak
- Sticky BBQ Baby Carrots
- Smoky Grilled Veggie Kebabs
- Spicy BBQ Cauliflower Wings
- Carolina Gold BBQ Pulled Chicken
- Grilled Cedar Plank Salmon
- Honey BBQ Sweet Potato Fries
- BBQ Meatball Skewers
- Grilled Romaine with Parmesan Dressing
- BBQ Pineapple Chicken Tacos
- Smoky BBQ Portobello Burgers
- Coffee-Rubbed Grilled Ribeye
- Charred BBQ Asparagus Bundles
- BBQ Beef Brisket Nachos
- Sweet & Spicy BBQ Tofu Skewers
- Grilled Peach and Burrata Salad
- BBQ Pork Belly Burnt Ends
- Garlic and Herb Grilled Mushrooms
- Chipotle Honey BBQ Drumsticks
- Grilled Watermelon with Feta and Mint
- Korean BBQ Short Ribs (Galbi)
- Smoky BBQ Black Bean Burgers
- Teriyaki BBQ Chicken Skewers
- Grilled Zucchini with Lemon Butter

- BBQ Pulled Pork Stuffed Bell Peppers
- Sticky Sweet BBQ Spareribs
- Smoky Grilled Eggplant Steaks
- BBQ Baked Beans with Bacon
- Spicy BBQ Sausage Links
- Grilled Mango Salsa with Chips
- BBQ Lamb Chops with Rosemary
- Honey-Mustard BBQ Glazed Salmon
- BBQ Chicken and Pineapple Pizza
- Grilled Flatbread with Smoky Hummus
- BBQ Pork Tenderloin with Apple Slaw
- Tangy BBQ Turkey Burgers
- BBQ Beef and Mushroom Skewers
- Grilled Avocado with Salsa Fresca
- Sweet Chili BBQ Pork Ribs

Classic BBQ Baby Back Ribs

Ingredients:

- 2 racks of baby back ribs
- 1 tablespoon olive oil
- 1 tablespoon salt
- 1 tablespoon black pepper
- 1 tablespoon garlic powder
- 1 tablespoon onion powder
- 1 teaspoon paprika
- 1 teaspoon chili powder (optional for a bit of heat)
- 1 teaspoon dried oregano
- 1 cup of BBQ sauce (your favorite brand or homemade)

Instructions:

1. **Preheat the Oven:** Preheat your oven to 275°F (135°C).
2. **Prepare the Ribs:** Remove the thin membrane from the back of the ribs by lifting it with a knife and pulling it off (it can be a bit tricky, but it's worth it for tender ribs).
3. **Season the Ribs:** Rub the ribs with olive oil, then season them generously with salt, pepper, garlic powder, onion powder, paprika, chili powder, and oregano. Massage the seasoning into the meat on both sides.
4. **Wrap and Bake:** Place each rack of ribs on a large piece of aluminum foil. Wrap them tightly and place them on a baking sheet. Bake in the preheated oven for 2.5 to 3 hours, or until the ribs are tender and cooked through.
5. **Grill (Optional for Crispiness):** Preheat your grill to medium-high heat. Remove the ribs from the oven, unwrap the foil, and brush your favorite BBQ sauce over the ribs. Place the ribs on the grill and cook for an additional 5–10 minutes, basting with more sauce and turning occasionally, until the sauce is caramelized and bubbly.
6. **Serve:** Remove the ribs from the grill, let them rest for a few minutes, then slice them into individual ribs. Serve with extra BBQ sauce on the side.

Grilled Garlic Butter Shrimp Skewers

Ingredients:

- 1 lb large shrimp, peeled and deveined
- 3 tablespoons unsalted butter, melted
- 3 cloves garlic, minced
- 1 tablespoon lemon juice
- 1 tablespoon olive oil
- Salt and pepper to taste
- 1 tablespoon fresh parsley, chopped

Instructions:

1. **Prepare the Marinade:** In a bowl, combine melted butter, minced garlic, lemon juice, olive oil, salt, and pepper.
2. **Marinate the Shrimp:** Toss the shrimp in the marinade, cover, and refrigerate for 15-20 minutes.
3. **Preheat Grill:** Preheat your grill to medium-high heat.
4. **Skewer the Shrimp:** Thread the shrimp onto skewers.
5. **Grill the Shrimp:** Place the skewers on the grill and cook for 2-3 minutes per side, or until the shrimp are opaque and slightly charred.
6. **Serve:** Sprinkle with fresh parsley and serve immediately.

Honey-Glazed BBQ Chicken Wings

Ingredients:

- 2 lbs chicken wings
- 1/4 cup honey
- 1/4 cup BBQ sauce
- 2 tablespoons soy sauce
- 1 tablespoon apple cider vinegar
- Salt and pepper to taste

Instructions:

1. **Prepare the Marinade:** In a bowl, whisk together honey, BBQ sauce, soy sauce, apple cider vinegar, salt, and pepper.
2. **Marinate the Wings:** Coat the chicken wings with the marinade and refrigerate for at least 1 hour.
3. **Preheat Grill:** Preheat your grill to medium heat.
4. **Grill the Wings:** Grill the wings for 20-25 minutes, turning occasionally until fully cooked and crispy.
5. **Serve:** Brush the wings with extra glaze before serving.

Smoky BBQ Pulled Pork Sliders

Ingredients:

- 2 lbs pork shoulder
- 1/4 cup BBQ dry rub (store-bought or homemade)
- 1/2 cup BBQ sauce
- 12 slider buns
- Coleslaw for topping (optional)

Instructions:

1. **Prepare the Pork:** Rub the pork shoulder with BBQ dry rub, then wrap it in foil and refrigerate for at least 4 hours or overnight.
2. **Cook the Pork:** Slow-cook the pork at 250°F for 6-8 hours until it is tender and easily shredded.
3. **Shred the Pork:** Remove the pork from the grill, shred it with two forks, and mix it with BBQ sauce.
4. **Assemble the Sliders:** Spoon the pulled pork onto slider buns and top with coleslaw, if desired.
5. **Serve:** Serve the sliders warm.

Sweet and Tangy Grilled Pineapple Rings

Ingredients:

- 1 fresh pineapple, peeled, cored, and cut into rings
- 2 tablespoons honey
- 1 tablespoon lime juice
- 1 teaspoon cinnamon

Instructions:

1. **Prepare the Pineapple:** Brush the pineapple rings with honey and lime juice.
2. **Preheat Grill:** Preheat the grill to medium heat.
3. **Grill the Pineapple:** Place the pineapple rings on the grill and cook for 3-4 minutes per side, or until grill marks appear.
4. **Serve:** Sprinkle with cinnamon and serve warm.

BBQ Brisket with Homemade Rub

Ingredients:

- 4-5 lb beef brisket
- 1/4 cup paprika
- 2 tablespoons brown sugar
- 1 tablespoon black pepper
- 1 tablespoon salt
- 1 tablespoon garlic powder
- 1 tablespoon onion powder
- 1 tablespoon chili powder
- 1 teaspoon cumin
- 1 teaspoon smoked paprika
- 1 cup BBQ sauce

Instructions:

1. **Prepare the Rub:** Combine all the dry ingredients in a small bowl.
2. **Season the Brisket:** Rub the brisket generously with the seasoning mixture.
3. **Cook the Brisket:** Slow-cook the brisket at 250°F for 4-5 hours, until tender.
4. **Glaze and Grill:** Brush the brisket with BBQ sauce and grill for 5-10 minutes, basting with more sauce.
5. **Serve:** Slice and serve the brisket with extra BBQ sauce.

Cajun-Spiced Grilled Corn on the Cob

Ingredients:

- 6 ears of corn, husked
- 1/4 cup olive oil
- 1 tablespoon Cajun seasoning
- 1 tablespoon smoked paprika
- 1 teaspoon garlic powder
- Salt and pepper to taste

Instructions:

1. **Prepare the Corn:** Brush the corn with olive oil, then sprinkle with Cajun seasoning, paprika, garlic powder, salt, and pepper.
2. **Preheat Grill:** Preheat the grill to medium-high heat.
3. **Grill the Corn:** Grill the corn for 10-12 minutes, turning occasionally until it is charred and tender.
4. **Serve:** Serve with extra seasoning if desired.

Maple-Bourbon BBQ Salmon Fillets

Ingredients:

- 4 salmon fillets
- 1/4 cup maple syrup
- 2 tablespoons bourbon
- 2 tablespoons soy sauce
- 1 tablespoon Dijon mustard
- 1 teaspoon garlic powder

Instructions:

1. **Prepare the Marinade:** Mix maple syrup, bourbon, soy sauce, Dijon mustard, and garlic powder in a bowl.
2. **Marinate the Salmon:** Coat the salmon fillets with the marinade and refrigerate for at least 30 minutes.
3. **Preheat Grill:** Preheat your grill to medium heat.
4. **Grill the Salmon:** Grill the salmon for 4-6 minutes per side, until cooked through.
5. **Serve:** Serve with extra marinade drizzled over the top.

Chipotle-Lime Grilled Pork Chops

Ingredients:

- 4 bone-in pork chops
- 2 tablespoons chipotle chili powder
- 1 tablespoon lime zest
- 2 tablespoons lime juice
- 2 cloves garlic, minced
- Salt and pepper to taste

Instructions:

1. **Prepare the Marinade:** In a bowl, combine chipotle chili powder, lime zest, lime juice, garlic, salt, and pepper.
2. **Marinate the Pork Chops:** Coat the pork chops with the marinade and refrigerate for at least 1 hour.
3. **Preheat Grill:** Preheat your grill to medium-high heat.
4. **Grill the Pork Chops:** Grill the pork chops for 5-7 minutes per side, or until fully cooked and golden brown.
5. **Serve:** Let the pork chops rest for a few minutes before serving.

Zesty BBQ Jackfruit Sandwiches

Ingredients:

- 2 cans young green jackfruit in brine, drained and shredded
- 1 tablespoon olive oil
- 1 onion, sliced
- 3 cloves garlic, minced
- 1 cup BBQ sauce (your favorite brand)
- 1 tablespoon apple cider vinegar
- 1 tablespoon brown sugar
- Salt and pepper to taste
- 8 slider buns
- Coleslaw for topping (optional)

Instructions:

1. **Prepare the Jackfruit:** Heat olive oil in a pan over medium heat. Add the onion and garlic, cooking until softened.
2. **Cook the Jackfruit:** Add the shredded jackfruit to the pan and stir to combine. Add BBQ sauce, apple cider vinegar, brown sugar, salt, and pepper. Cook for 10-15 minutes, stirring occasionally until the mixture thickens.
3. **Assemble the Sandwiches:** Spoon the BBQ jackfruit onto slider buns and top with coleslaw, if desired.
4. **Serve:** Serve the sandwiches warm.

BBQ Bacon-Wrapped Jalapeño Poppers

Ingredients:

- 12 large jalapeño peppers, halved and seeded
- 8 oz cream cheese, softened
- 1/2 cup shredded cheddar cheese
- 1/2 teaspoon garlic powder
- 12 slices bacon, cut in half
- 1/4 cup BBQ sauce

Instructions:

1. **Prepare the Filling:** In a bowl, mix the cream cheese, cheddar cheese, garlic powder, salt, and pepper.
2. **Stuff the Peppers:** Fill each jalapeño half with the cheese mixture.
3. **Wrap with Bacon:** Wrap each stuffed jalapeño with half a slice of bacon and secure with toothpicks.
4. **Grill:** Preheat the grill to medium heat. Grill the bacon-wrapped poppers for 10-12 minutes, turning occasionally, until the bacon is crispy.
5. **Serve:** Brush with BBQ sauce and serve hot.

Herb-Grilled Flat Iron Steak

Ingredients:

- 2 flat iron steaks
- 2 tablespoons olive oil
- 2 tablespoons fresh rosemary, chopped
- 2 tablespoons fresh thyme, chopped
- 2 cloves garlic, minced
- Salt and pepper to taste

Instructions:

1. **Prepare the Marinade:** In a bowl, mix olive oil, rosemary, thyme, garlic, salt, and pepper.
2. **Marinate the Steaks:** Rub the marinade over the steaks and refrigerate for 30 minutes to 1 hour.
3. **Preheat the Grill:** Preheat the grill to medium-high heat.
4. **Grill the Steaks:** Grill the steaks for 4-5 minutes per side for medium-rare, or longer for your preferred doneness.
5. **Serve:** Let the steaks rest for a few minutes before slicing and serving.

Sticky BBQ Baby Carrots

Ingredients:

- 1 lb baby carrots, peeled
- 2 tablespoons olive oil
- 1/4 cup honey
- 1/4 cup BBQ sauce
- Salt and pepper to taste
- 1 tablespoon fresh parsley, chopped (optional)

Instructions:

1. **Prepare the Carrots:** Toss the baby carrots in olive oil, salt, and pepper.
2. **Grill the Carrots:** Preheat the grill to medium heat. Grill the carrots for 8-10 minutes, turning occasionally until tender.
3. **Make the Glaze:** In a small bowl, mix honey and BBQ sauce.
4. **Glaze the Carrots:** Brush the glaze onto the carrots during the last 2-3 minutes of grilling.
5. **Serve:** Remove from the grill, sprinkle with fresh parsley if desired, and serve.

Smoky Grilled Veggie Kebabs

Ingredients:

- 1 red bell pepper, cut into chunks
- 1 yellow bell pepper, cut into chunks
- 1 zucchini, sliced
- 1 red onion, cut into chunks
- 1 cup cherry tomatoes
- 1/4 cup olive oil
- 2 tablespoons balsamic vinegar
- 1 teaspoon smoked paprika
- Salt and pepper to taste

Instructions:

1. **Prepare the Vegetables:** Thread the vegetables onto skewers, alternating between different veggies.
2. **Make the Marinade:** In a small bowl, whisk together olive oil, balsamic vinegar, smoked paprika, salt, and pepper.
3. **Marinate the Veggies:** Brush the vegetables with the marinade and let them sit for 15-20 minutes.
4. **Grill the Kebabs:** Preheat the grill to medium-high heat. Grill the kebabs for 8-10 minutes, turning occasionally, until the vegetables are tender and slightly charred.
5. **Serve:** Serve the veggie kebabs warm.

Spicy BBQ Cauliflower Wings

Ingredients:

- 1 head of cauliflower, cut into florets
- 1 cup flour
- 1 cup water
- 1 teaspoon paprika
- 1 teaspoon garlic powder
- Salt and pepper to taste
- 1 cup BBQ sauce
- 1 tablespoon hot sauce (optional)

Instructions:

1. **Prepare the Batter:** In a bowl, whisk together flour, water, paprika, garlic powder, salt, and pepper to form a batter.
2. **Coat the Cauliflower:** Dip each cauliflower floret into the batter, coating evenly.
3. **Bake the Cauliflower:** Preheat your oven to 400°F (200°C). Place the cauliflower on a baking sheet lined with parchment paper and bake for 25-30 minutes until crispy.
4. **Make the Sauce:** In a small bowl, mix BBQ sauce with hot sauce (if using).
5. **Glaze and Serve:** Brush the baked cauliflower wings with the BBQ sauce mixture and bake for an additional 5-10 minutes. Serve hot.

Carolina Gold BBQ Pulled Chicken

Ingredients:

- 2 lbs chicken breasts
- 1/2 cup Carolina Gold BBQ sauce (mustard-based)
- 2 tablespoons apple cider vinegar
- 1 tablespoon honey
- Salt and pepper to taste
- 8 buns for serving

Instructions:

1. **Cook the Chicken:** In a slow cooker or on the stovetop, cook the chicken with a little water until fully cooked and easily shredded.
2. **Shred the Chicken:** Shred the chicken with two forks.
3. **Make the Sauce:** In a bowl, mix the Carolina Gold BBQ sauce, apple cider vinegar, honey, salt, and pepper.
4. **Combine the Chicken and Sauce:** Toss the shredded chicken with the BBQ sauce mixture.
5. **Serve:** Spoon the pulled chicken onto buns and serve immediately.

Grilled Cedar Plank Salmon

Ingredients:

- 4 salmon fillets
- 2 cedar planks (soaked in water for at least 1 hour)
- 2 tablespoons olive oil
- 1 tablespoon lemon juice
- 2 cloves garlic, minced
- Salt and pepper to taste

Instructions:

1. **Prepare the Planks:** Preheat the grill to medium heat. Place the soaked cedar planks on the grill to heat for 5 minutes.
2. **Prepare the Salmon:** Brush the salmon fillets with olive oil, lemon juice, garlic, salt, and pepper.
3. **Grill the Salmon:** Place the salmon fillets on the heated cedar planks and grill for 12-15 minutes, until the salmon is cooked through.
4. **Serve:** Serve the salmon directly from the cedar planks for a smoky flavor.

Honey BBQ Sweet Potato Fries

Ingredients:

- 2 large sweet potatoes, peeled and cut into fries
- 2 tablespoons olive oil
- Salt and pepper to taste
- 1/4 cup BBQ sauce
- 2 tablespoons honey
- Fresh parsley for garnish (optional)

Instructions:

1. **Preheat Oven:** Preheat the oven to 425°F (220°C). Line a baking sheet with parchment paper.
2. **Prepare the Fries:** Toss the sweet potato fries in olive oil, salt, and pepper. Spread them out in a single layer on the baking sheet.
3. **Bake the Fries:** Bake for 20-25 minutes, flipping halfway through, until the fries are crispy and golden brown.
4. **Make the Glaze:** In a small saucepan, combine BBQ sauce and honey. Heat over low heat until warm.
5. **Toss and Serve:** Drizzle the honey BBQ glaze over the baked fries and toss to coat. Garnish with fresh parsley if desired.

BBQ Meatball Skewers

Ingredients:

- 1 lb ground beef or turkey
- 1/4 cup breadcrumbs
- 1/4 cup grated Parmesan cheese
- 1 egg
- 2 cloves garlic, minced
- 1 teaspoon dried oregano
- Salt and pepper to taste
- 1/2 cup BBQ sauce
- Skewers (wooden or metal)

Instructions:

1. **Make the Meatballs:** In a bowl, combine ground meat, breadcrumbs, Parmesan cheese, egg, garlic, oregano, salt, and pepper. Form into small meatballs, about 1 inch in diameter.
2. **Skewer the Meatballs:** Thread the meatballs onto skewers.
3. **Grill the Meatballs:** Preheat the grill to medium heat. Grill the meatballs for 8-10 minutes, turning occasionally, until cooked through.
4. **Glaze with BBQ Sauce:** Brush the meatballs with BBQ sauce during the last 2-3 minutes of grilling.
5. **Serve:** Serve the meatball skewers warm, with extra BBQ sauce on the side for dipping.

Grilled Romaine with Parmesan Dressing

Ingredients:

- 2 heads romaine lettuce, halved lengthwise
- 2 tablespoons olive oil
- Salt and pepper to taste
- 1/4 cup grated Parmesan cheese
- 2 tablespoons Caesar dressing

Instructions:

1. **Prepare the Lettuce:** Brush the cut sides of the romaine lettuce with olive oil and season with salt and pepper.
2. **Grill the Lettuce:** Preheat the grill to medium heat. Place the lettuce halves cut-side down on the grill and cook for 2-3 minutes until charred and slightly wilted.
3. **Dress and Serve:** Drizzle the grilled romaine with Caesar dressing and sprinkle with Parmesan cheese before serving.

BBQ Pineapple Chicken Tacos

Ingredients:

- 2 chicken breasts, grilled and shredded
- 1 cup BBQ sauce
- 1 cup fresh pineapple, diced
- 1/4 cup red onion, finely chopped
- 1 tablespoon cilantro, chopped
- 8 small taco tortillas
- Lime wedges for serving

Instructions:

1. **Grill the Chicken:** Grill the chicken breasts over medium heat for 6-8 minutes per side, until fully cooked. Shred the chicken once cooked.
2. **Make the Pineapple Salsa:** In a bowl, combine the pineapple, red onion, and cilantro.
3. **Combine with BBQ Sauce:** Toss the shredded chicken in BBQ sauce and mix until coated.
4. **Assemble the Tacos:** Warm the tortillas and spoon the BBQ chicken into each one. Top with pineapple salsa and a squeeze of lime juice.
5. **Serve:** Serve the tacos immediately.

Smoky BBQ Portobello Burgers

Ingredients:

- 4 large portobello mushroom caps, stems removed
- 1/4 cup olive oil
- 2 tablespoons balsamic vinegar
- 1 teaspoon smoked paprika
- Salt and pepper to taste
- 4 burger buns
- BBQ sauce
- Fresh lettuce, tomato, and cheese for toppings

Instructions:

1. **Marinate the Mushrooms:** In a bowl, whisk together olive oil, balsamic vinegar, smoked paprika, salt, and pepper. Coat the mushroom caps in the marinade and let sit for 15 minutes.
2. **Grill the Mushrooms:** Preheat the grill to medium heat. Grill the mushrooms for 5-7 minutes per side until tender.
3. **Assemble the Burgers:** Toast the buns on the grill, then place a grilled portobello cap on each bun. Top with BBQ sauce, lettuce, tomato, and cheese.
4. **Serve:** Serve the portobello burgers immediately.

Coffee-Rubbed Grilled Ribeye

Ingredients:

- 2 ribeye steaks
- 2 tablespoons ground coffee
- 1 tablespoon brown sugar
- 1 tablespoon smoked paprika
- 1 teaspoon garlic powder
- Salt and pepper to taste

Instructions:

1. **Make the Coffee Rub:** In a small bowl, combine ground coffee, brown sugar, smoked paprika, garlic powder, salt, and pepper.
2. **Rub the Steaks:** Coat the ribeye steaks with the coffee rub, pressing gently to adhere.
3. **Grill the Steaks:** Preheat the grill to high heat. Grill the steaks for 4-5 minutes per side for medium-rare, or longer for your preferred doneness.
4. **Rest and Serve:** Let the steaks rest for a few minutes before slicing and serving.

Charred BBQ Asparagus Bundles

Ingredients:

- 1 bunch asparagus, trimmed
- 1 tablespoon olive oil
- Salt and pepper to taste
- 4 slices bacon, cooked and crumbled
- 1/4 cup BBQ sauce

Instructions:

1. **Prepare the Asparagus:** Group 4-5 asparagus stalks together and tie them with a slice of bacon.
2. **Grill the Bundles:** Preheat the grill to medium-high heat. Grill the asparagus bundles for 4-6 minutes, turning occasionally until tender and slightly charred.
3. **Brush with BBQ Sauce:** During the last minute of grilling, brush the bundles with BBQ sauce.
4. **Serve:** Remove the asparagus bundles from the grill and serve immediately.

BBQ Beef Brisket Nachos

Ingredients:

- 1 lb cooked BBQ beef brisket, shredded
- Tortilla chips
- 1 cup shredded cheddar cheese
- 1/2 cup sliced jalapeños
- 1/4 cup diced red onion
- 1/4 cup BBQ sauce
- Sour cream for garnish (optional)
- Fresh cilantro for garnish (optional)

Instructions:

1. **Prepare the Nachos:** Preheat the oven to 375°F (190°C). Spread tortilla chips on a baking sheet.
2. **Assemble the Nachos:** Top the chips with shredded BBQ brisket, cheddar cheese, jalapeños, and red onion.
3. **Bake the Nachos:** Bake for 10-12 minutes, until the cheese is melted and bubbly.
4. **Finish and Serve:** Drizzle with BBQ sauce and garnish with sour cream and cilantro. Serve hot.

Sweet & Spicy BBQ Tofu Skewers

Ingredients:

- 1 block firm tofu, pressed and cubed
- 1/4 cup BBQ sauce
- 2 tablespoons honey
- 1 tablespoon sriracha sauce
- 1 tablespoon soy sauce
- 1 tablespoon olive oil
- Salt and pepper to taste
- Skewers (wooden or metal)

Instructions:

1. **Prepare the Marinade:** In a bowl, mix BBQ sauce, honey, sriracha sauce, soy sauce, olive oil, salt, and pepper.
2. **Marinate the Tofu:** Toss the tofu cubes in the marinade and let sit for at least 30 minutes.
3. **Skewer the Tofu:** Thread the marinated tofu onto skewers.
4. **Grill the Skewers:** Preheat the grill to medium heat. Grill the tofu skewers for 6-8 minutes, turning occasionally until golden and slightly crispy on the edges.
5. **Serve:** Serve the sweet and spicy BBQ tofu skewers immediately.

Grilled Peach and Burrata Salad

Ingredients:

- 4 ripe peaches, halved and pitted
- 2 tablespoons olive oil
- Salt and pepper to taste
- 1 ball burrata cheese
- 2 cups arugula or mixed greens
- 1 tablespoon balsamic vinegar
- Honey for drizzling (optional)

Instructions:

1. **Prepare the Peaches:** Brush the peach halves with olive oil and season with salt and pepper.
2. **Grill the Peaches:** Preheat the grill to medium heat. Grill the peaches for 3-4 minutes per side, until grill marks appear and the peaches soften.
3. **Assemble the Salad:** Arrange the arugula or mixed greens on a platter. Tear the burrata into pieces and place it on top of the greens.
4. **Add the Peaches:** Add the grilled peaches to the salad.
5. **Finish and Serve:** Drizzle with balsamic vinegar and honey (optional) before serving.

BBQ Pork Belly Burnt Ends

Ingredients:

- 2 lbs pork belly, cut into 1-inch cubes
- 1/4 cup brown sugar
- 2 tablespoons paprika
- 1 tablespoon garlic powder
- 1 tablespoon onion powder
- 1 teaspoon smoked paprika
- Salt and pepper to taste
- 1/2 cup BBQ sauce

Instructions:

1. **Prepare the Pork Belly:** Preheat the grill to 250°F (120°C). In a bowl, combine brown sugar, paprika, garlic powder, onion powder, smoked paprika, salt, and pepper.
2. **Season the Pork Belly:** Rub the spice mixture generously over the pork belly cubes.
3. **Smoke the Pork Belly:** Place the pork belly cubes on the grill and smoke for 2-3 hours, turning occasionally until the cubes are tender.
4. **Coat with BBQ Sauce:** After smoking, toss the burnt ends in BBQ sauce and cook for an additional 20-30 minutes until caramelized.
5. **Serve:** Serve the BBQ pork belly burnt ends hot.

Garlic and Herb Grilled Mushrooms

Ingredients:

- 16 oz button mushrooms, cleaned and stems removed
- 3 tablespoons olive oil
- 2 tablespoons garlic, minced
- 1 tablespoon fresh thyme, chopped
- 1 tablespoon fresh rosemary, chopped
- Salt and pepper to taste
- Lemon wedges for serving

Instructions:

1. **Prepare the Marinade:** In a bowl, mix olive oil, garlic, thyme, rosemary, salt, and pepper.
2. **Marinate the Mushrooms:** Toss the mushrooms in the marinade and let sit for 10-15 minutes.
3. **Grill the Mushrooms:** Preheat the grill to medium heat. Grill the mushrooms for 3-4 minutes per side, until tender and slightly charred.
4. **Serve:** Serve with a squeeze of fresh lemon juice.

Chipotle Honey BBQ Drumsticks

Ingredients:

- 8 chicken drumsticks
- 1/4 cup BBQ sauce
- 2 tablespoons honey
- 1 tablespoon chipotle peppers in adobo sauce, minced
- 1 tablespoon olive oil
- Salt and pepper to taste

Instructions:

1. **Prepare the Marinade:** In a bowl, combine BBQ sauce, honey, chipotle peppers, olive oil, salt, and pepper.
2. **Marinate the Drumsticks:** Coat the chicken drumsticks in the marinade and let sit for at least 30 minutes.
3. **Grill the Drumsticks:** Preheat the grill to medium heat. Grill the drumsticks for 25-30 minutes, turning occasionally, until fully cooked and crispy on the outside.
4. **Serve:** Serve the chipotle honey BBQ drumsticks hot.

Grilled Watermelon with Feta and Mint

Ingredients:

- 4 thick slices of watermelon
- 1 tablespoon olive oil
- 1/2 cup crumbled feta cheese
- Fresh mint leaves, chopped
- Balsamic glaze for drizzling

Instructions:

1. **Prepare the Watermelon:** Brush the watermelon slices with olive oil.
2. **Grill the Watermelon:** Preheat the grill to medium heat. Grill the watermelon slices for 2-3 minutes per side, just until grill marks appear.
3. **Assemble the Salad:** Top the grilled watermelon with crumbled feta cheese and chopped mint.
4. **Finish and Serve:** Drizzle with balsamic glaze before serving.

Korean BBQ Short Ribs (Galbi)

Ingredients:

- 2 lbs beef short ribs, thinly sliced
- 1/4 cup soy sauce
- 2 tablespoons sesame oil
- 2 tablespoons brown sugar
- 3 cloves garlic, minced
- 1 tablespoon grated ginger
- 1 tablespoon rice vinegar
- 1 tablespoon gochujang (Korean chili paste)
- 1/4 cup green onions, chopped
- Sesame seeds for garnish

Instructions:

1. **Prepare the Marinade:** In a bowl, whisk together soy sauce, sesame oil, brown sugar, garlic, ginger, rice vinegar, gochujang, and green onions.
2. **Marinate the Short Ribs:** Place the short ribs in a resealable bag or shallow dish and pour the marinade over them. Let marinate for at least 2 hours or overnight for more flavor.
3. **Grill the Short Ribs:** Preheat the grill to medium-high heat. Grill the short ribs for 2-3 minutes per side, until caramelized and cooked through.
4. **Serve:** Garnish with sesame seeds and additional green onions before serving.

Smoky BBQ Black Bean Burgers

Ingredients:

- 1 can (15 oz) black beans, drained and mashed
- 1/4 cup breadcrumbs
- 1/4 cup grated carrot
- 1/4 cup chopped onion
- 1 tablespoon smoked paprika
- 1 teaspoon garlic powder
- Salt and pepper to taste
- Olive oil for grilling
- Burger buns and toppings (lettuce, tomato, etc.)

Instructions:

1. **Make the Burger Patties:** In a bowl, combine mashed black beans, breadcrumbs, grated carrot, chopped onion, smoked paprika, garlic powder, salt, and pepper. Mix until well combined. Form into patties.
2. **Grill the Patties:** Preheat the grill to medium heat. Lightly brush the patties with olive oil and grill for 4-5 minutes per side, until golden and crispy.
3. **Assemble the Burgers:** Place the grilled black bean patties on burger buns and add your favorite toppings.
4. **Serve:** Serve the smoky BBQ black bean burgers immediately.

Teriyaki BBQ Chicken Skewers

Ingredients:

- 2 lbs chicken breast or thighs, cut into bite-sized cubes
- 1/4 cup soy sauce
- 2 tablespoons honey
- 2 tablespoons rice vinegar
- 2 tablespoons brown sugar
- 2 teaspoons grated ginger
- 2 cloves garlic, minced
- 1 tablespoon sesame oil
- 1 tablespoon cornstarch (optional, for thickening)
- Skewers (wooden or metal)

Instructions:

1. **Make the Marinade:** In a bowl, combine soy sauce, honey, rice vinegar, brown sugar, ginger, garlic, sesame oil, and cornstarch (if using).
2. **Marinate the Chicken:** Place the chicken cubes in the marinade and let it sit for at least 30 minutes, or up to 2 hours in the fridge.
3. **Skewer the Chicken:** Thread the marinated chicken onto the skewers.
4. **Grill the Skewers:** Preheat the grill to medium-high heat. Grill the chicken skewers for 6-8 minutes per side, until cooked through and lightly charred.
5. **Serve:** Serve the Teriyaki BBQ chicken skewers hot, garnished with sesame seeds and green onions if desired.

Grilled Zucchini with Lemon Butter

Ingredients:

- 4 zucchinis, sliced lengthwise
- 2 tablespoons olive oil
- Salt and pepper to taste
- 3 tablespoons unsalted butter, melted
- 1 teaspoon lemon zest
- 1 tablespoon fresh lemon juice
- Fresh parsley for garnish

Instructions:

1. **Prepare the Zucchini:** Preheat the grill to medium heat. Brush the zucchini slices with olive oil and season with salt and pepper.
2. **Grill the Zucchini:** Place the zucchini on the grill and cook for 3-4 minutes per side, until tender and slightly charred.
3. **Make the Lemon Butter:** In a small bowl, mix the melted butter, lemon zest, and lemon juice.
4. **Serve:** Drizzle the lemon butter over the grilled zucchini and garnish with fresh parsley.

BBQ Pulled Pork Stuffed Bell Peppers

Ingredients:

- 4 large bell peppers, tops cut off and seeds removed
- 2 cups cooked pulled pork
- 1/4 cup BBQ sauce
- 1/2 cup shredded cheddar cheese
- 1/4 cup green onions, chopped

Instructions:

1. **Preheat the Grill:** Heat the grill to medium heat.
2. **Prepare the Peppers:** Stuff each bell pepper with pulled pork and drizzle with BBQ sauce.
3. **Grill the Peppers:** Place the stuffed peppers on the grill and cook for 10-15 minutes, until the peppers are tender and the filling is heated through.
4. **Top with Cheese:** Sprinkle shredded cheddar cheese on top of the stuffed peppers and grill for an additional 2-3 minutes until the cheese melts.
5. **Serve:** Garnish with chopped green onions before serving.

Sticky Sweet BBQ Spareribs

Ingredients:

- 2 racks of baby back ribs
- 1/2 cup BBQ sauce
- 1/4 cup honey
- 1 tablespoon soy sauce
- 1 tablespoon apple cider vinegar
- 1 teaspoon garlic powder
- 1 teaspoon smoked paprika
- Salt and pepper to taste

Instructions:

1. **Preheat the Grill:** Preheat your grill to medium heat.
2. **Prepare the Ribs:** Remove the membrane from the back of the ribs. Season the ribs with salt, pepper, garlic powder, and smoked paprika.
3. **Grill the Ribs:** Grill the ribs for 1.5-2 hours, turning occasionally to prevent burning, until the ribs are tender.
4. **Make the BBQ Sauce:** In a saucepan, combine BBQ sauce, honey, soy sauce, and apple cider vinegar. Simmer for 10 minutes until thickened.
5. **Glaze and Serve:** During the last 15 minutes of grilling, baste the ribs with the sticky BBQ sauce. Serve the ribs with extra sauce on the side.

Smoky Grilled Eggplant Steaks

Ingredients:

- 2 large eggplants, sliced into 1-inch thick steaks
- 2 tablespoons olive oil
- 1 tablespoon smoked paprika
- 1 teaspoon garlic powder
- Salt and pepper to taste
- Fresh basil for garnish

Instructions:

1. **Prepare the Eggplant:** Brush the eggplant steaks with olive oil and season with smoked paprika, garlic powder, salt, and pepper.
2. **Grill the Eggplant:** Preheat the grill to medium heat. Grill the eggplant steaks for 4-5 minutes per side, until tender and lightly charred.
3. **Serve:** Garnish the grilled eggplant with fresh basil before serving.

BBQ Baked Beans with Bacon

Ingredients:

- 1 can (28 oz) baked beans
- 1/2 cup BBQ sauce
- 1/4 cup brown sugar
- 1 tablespoon Worcestershire sauce
- 1/2 teaspoon smoked paprika
- 6 slices bacon, cooked and crumbled
- 1/4 cup onion, finely chopped

Instructions:

1. **Prepare the Beans:** In a saucepan, combine the baked beans, BBQ sauce, brown sugar, Worcestershire sauce, and smoked paprika.
2. **Cook the Bacon:** Cook the bacon in a skillet until crispy, then crumble and set aside.
3. **Simmer the Beans:** Bring the bean mixture to a simmer over medium heat, stirring occasionally. Let cook for 10-15 minutes.
4. **Add Bacon:** Stir in the crumbled bacon and onion. Simmer for an additional 5 minutes.
5. **Serve:** Serve the BBQ baked beans hot.

Spicy BBQ Sausage Links

Ingredients:

- 8 spicy sausage links (like chorizo or Italian sausage)
- 1/4 cup BBQ sauce
- 1 tablespoon hot sauce (optional)
- 1 teaspoon smoked paprika
- Fresh cilantro for garnish

Instructions:

1. **Preheat the Grill:** Preheat the grill to medium-high heat.
2. **Grill the Sausages:** Grill the sausages for 8-10 minutes, turning occasionally, until fully cooked.
3. **Prepare the Sauce:** In a small bowl, combine BBQ sauce, hot sauce (if using), and smoked paprika.
4. **Glaze the Sausages:** During the last 2-3 minutes of grilling, brush the sausages with the BBQ sauce mixture.
5. **Serve:** Garnish with fresh cilantro before serving.

Grilled Mango Salsa with Chips

Ingredients:

- 2 ripe mangoes, peeled and diced
- 1/2 red onion, finely chopped
- 1/4 cup cilantro, chopped
- 1 jalapeño, finely chopped (optional)
- Juice of 1 lime
- Salt and pepper to taste
- Tortilla chips for serving

Instructions:

1. **Grill the Mango:** Preheat the grill to medium heat. Grill the mango slices for 2-3 minutes per side, just to get grill marks.
2. **Make the Salsa:** Dice the grilled mango and combine it in a bowl with onion, cilantro, jalapeño (if using), lime juice, salt, and pepper.
3. **Serve:** Serve the grilled mango salsa with tortilla chips.

BBQ Lamb Chops with Rosemary

Ingredients:

- 8 lamb chops
- 3 tablespoons olive oil
- 2 tablespoons fresh rosemary, chopped
- 4 cloves garlic, minced
- 1 teaspoon lemon zest
- Salt and pepper to taste

Instructions:

1. **Marinate the Lamb:** In a bowl, mix olive oil, rosemary, garlic, lemon zest, salt, and pepper. Rub this marinade all over the lamb chops and let them marinate for at least 30 minutes.
2. **Preheat the Grill:** Preheat the grill to medium-high heat.
3. **Grill the Lamb Chops:** Grill the lamb chops for about 4-5 minutes per side, or until they reach your desired level of doneness.
4. **Serve:** Serve the BBQ lamb chops with additional rosemary and lemon wedges on the side.

Honey-Mustard BBQ Glazed Salmon

Ingredients:

- 4 salmon fillets
- 2 tablespoons Dijon mustard
- 2 tablespoons honey
- 1 tablespoon apple cider vinegar
- 1 teaspoon garlic powder
- Salt and pepper to taste

Instructions:

1. **Make the Glaze:** In a small bowl, whisk together Dijon mustard, honey, apple cider vinegar, garlic powder, salt, and pepper.
2. **Prepare the Salmon:** Brush the salmon fillets with the honey-mustard glaze on both sides.
3. **Grill the Salmon:** Preheat the grill to medium heat. Grill the salmon for 4-5 minutes per side, until cooked through and lightly charred.
4. **Serve:** Serve the glazed salmon hot, garnished with fresh herbs if desired.

BBQ Chicken and Pineapple Pizza

Ingredients:

- 1 pizza dough (store-bought or homemade)
- 1/2 cup BBQ sauce
- 1 chicken breast, cooked and shredded
- 1/2 cup pineapple chunks, drained
- 1/2 red onion, thinly sliced
- 1 cup shredded mozzarella cheese
- Fresh cilantro for garnish

Instructions:

1. **Preheat the Grill:** Preheat the grill to medium-high heat.
2. **Prepare the Pizza:** Roll out the pizza dough on a floured surface. Spread BBQ sauce over the dough, then top with shredded chicken, pineapple chunks, red onion, and mozzarella cheese.
3. **Grill the Pizza:** Place the pizza on the grill and cook for about 10-12 minutes, until the crust is crispy and the cheese is melted.
4. **Serve:** Garnish with fresh cilantro and serve immediately.

Grilled Flatbread with Smoky Hummus

Ingredients:

- 2 flatbreads
- 1 cup smoky hummus (store-bought or homemade)
- Olive oil for brushing
- Fresh parsley for garnish
- Paprika for sprinkling

Instructions:

1. **Grill the Flatbreads:** Preheat the grill to medium-high heat. Brush the flatbreads with olive oil and grill for 2-3 minutes per side until crispy and golden.
2. **Serve:** Spread a generous amount of smoky hummus over the grilled flatbreads and garnish with fresh parsley and a sprinkle of paprika.

BBQ Pork Tenderloin with Apple Slaw

Ingredients:

- 1 pork tenderloin
- 2 tablespoons olive oil
- 2 tablespoons BBQ sauce
- Salt and pepper to taste
- 1/2 head green cabbage, shredded
- 1 apple, julienned
- 1/4 cup mayonnaise
- 1 tablespoon apple cider vinegar
- 1 teaspoon honey

Instructions:

1. **Prepare the Pork Tenderloin:** Preheat the grill to medium-high heat. Rub the pork tenderloin with olive oil, BBQ sauce, salt, and pepper.
2. **Grill the Pork:** Grill the pork tenderloin for 20-25 minutes, turning occasionally, until the internal temperature reaches 145°F. Let it rest before slicing.
3. **Make the Apple Slaw:** In a bowl, combine the shredded cabbage, apple, mayonnaise, apple cider vinegar, and honey. Mix well.
4. **Serve:** Serve the grilled pork tenderloin with a side of apple slaw.

Tangy BBQ Turkey Burgers

Ingredients:

- 1 lb ground turkey
- 1/4 cup BBQ sauce
- 1/4 cup breadcrumbs
- 1/4 cup red onion, finely chopped
- Salt and pepper to taste
- 4 burger buns
- Lettuce, tomato, and pickles for garnish

Instructions:

1. **Prepare the Turkey Patties:** In a bowl, mix the ground turkey, BBQ sauce, breadcrumbs, red onion, salt, and pepper. Form into 4 burger patties.
2. **Grill the Patties:** Preheat the grill to medium heat. Grill the turkey patties for 5-7 minutes per side, until cooked through.
3. **Serve:** Place the cooked patties on burger buns and garnish with lettuce, tomato, and pickles.

BBQ Beef and Mushroom Skewers

Ingredients:

- 1 lb beef sirloin, cut into cubes
- 1/2 lb mushrooms, halved
- 1/4 cup olive oil
- 1/4 cup BBQ sauce
- 1 tablespoon soy sauce
- Salt and pepper to taste
- Skewers

Instructions:

1. **Prepare the Skewers:** Preheat the grill to medium-high heat. Thread the beef and mushrooms onto the skewers.
2. **Make the Marinade:** In a bowl, combine olive oil, BBQ sauce, soy sauce, salt, and pepper. Brush the skewers with the marinade.
3. **Grill the Skewers:** Grill the skewers for 4-5 minutes per side, until the beef is cooked to your desired doneness and the mushrooms are tender.
4. **Serve:** Serve the skewers hot.

Grilled Avocado with Salsa Fresca

Ingredients:

- 4 ripe avocados, halved and pitted
- 1 cup salsa fresca (fresh tomato, onion, cilantro, lime juice)
- Olive oil for drizzling
- Salt and pepper to taste

Instructions:

1. **Prepare the Avocados:** Preheat the grill to medium-high heat. Drizzle the avocado halves with olive oil and season with salt and pepper.
2. **Grill the Avocados:** Grill the avocado halves for 2-3 minutes per side, until slightly charred.
3. **Serve:** Top with fresh salsa fresca and serve immediately.

Sweet Chili BBQ Pork Ribs

Ingredients:

- 2 racks baby back ribs
- 1/4 cup BBQ sauce
- 1/4 cup sweet chili sauce
- 1 tablespoon soy sauce
- 1 tablespoon honey
- 2 cloves garlic, minced
- Salt and pepper to taste

Instructions:

1. **Preheat the Grill:** Preheat the grill to medium-high heat.
2. **Prepare the Ribs:** Remove the membrane from the back of the ribs and season with salt and pepper.
3. **Make the Glaze:** In a small bowl, combine BBQ sauce, sweet chili sauce, soy sauce, honey, and garlic. Brush the ribs with this sauce mixture.
4. **Grill the Ribs:** Grill the ribs for 1.5-2 hours, turning occasionally, and basting with the sauce. Serve hot.

www.ingramcontent.com/pod-product-compliance
Lightning Source LLC
LaVergne TN
LVHW081503060526
838201LV00056BA/2911